Chalo Sulky Handbook

Train Your Dog to love to pull a Sulky

Daphne Lewis

ISBN: 978-1-257-90950-6

Cover Photo:

Mark Acciavatti and his akita, Medusa, took to the sand dunes of New Jersey to create this photo on a warm summer's day. Mark normally runs Medusa in the cool of the morning when the air comes off the Atlantic Ocean, the low sun glistens on the water, and a hint of salt is in the air. The two of them run the sulky on the boardwalks and sidewalks of the New Jersey Shore. When you see them driving along, you understand a man, a sulky, and his best friend enjoying their time together.

Mike Szach, Photographer

Zaknj@hotmail.com

INTRODUCTION

A sulky dog must be well-trained so you and he are safe. It takes time, and he needs the following habits and skills.

1.   <u>Basic obedience</u>: Wait, stay, sit, stand.

1.   <u>Face forward</u> without moving when hitched.

2.   <u>Pull</u> on command.

3.   <u>Stop</u> on command.

4.   Walk, Trot, or Run on command.

5.   <u>Turn</u> right and left on command.

6.   <u>Stay to the right</u> on a wide trail. Change sides as commanded.

7.   <u>Avoid distractions</u> such as loose dogs.

1.   BASIC OBEDIENCE: STAY, SIT, STAND, WAIT.

I use "wait" for "whoa" because my dogs already know the word and because "whoa" sounds like "go" and "no." When I say, "wait," my dogs put on the brakes. They may turn their heads to look at me after they stop, but they still face forward. "Sit" is useful when the dogs are likely to disobey the "Stay" command. "Stand and stay" is essential when you are putting the harness on. It is especially essential when you are attaching a second dog to the sulky.

2.   FACE FORWARD WHEN HITCHED.

Dogs must face forward. The command to get them to face forward is "Line Out." This term is used by people whose dogs are pulling scooters, bikes, or sleds with a tug line. It means "hold the line out tight," which effectively means "walk forward until the line is tight and then stop and hold it there." The term is also useful for sulkies. You need the dog to stay there while you walk to the seat and sit down. The dog(s) must not consider your sitting down as a command to pull. They stand until you command them to pull.

3. PULL.

The dog must pull when you tell him "Pull" or "Walk." Usually the dog is eager to change from standing and waiting to going forward down the trail.

4. STOP/WAIT/WHOA.

It is obviously necessary for the dog to stop on command. Say the command once. If the dog does not stop on one command, use the brakes to enforce stop. I use "Wait."

5. WALK, TROT, AND RUN.

One of the great pleasures of driving a sulky is the teamwork. A dog that changes gaits on command will thrill you. In addition, it allows you to look after his well-being. For example, you may command "Walk" if you think he is overheating. You may command "Trot" on pavement, and "Hike" when on a dirt-paved straightaway. I use the word "Squirrels!" to speed my dogs up.

6. TURN RIGHT AND LEFT.

I use "gee" for "right" and "haw" for left, but you can use "right" and "left" if you prefer. The reins help you micromanage the turns, and they also help reinforce the turn command. Sometimes, I have to leap out of the sulky and pull on the reins to enforce my turn commands.

7. STAY TO THE RIGHT.

You will need to travel on the right on busy trails. To pass someone slower than you, such as a pedestrian, you will need to command the dog to move over to the left side of the trail.

8   IGNORE DISTRACTIONS.

A working dog ignores distractions and keeps on going. Distractions include bushes to pee on, wild animals, and loose dogs.

Once in harness, the dog is working and should not play or go say hi.

THE CHALO SULKY HARNESS

The harness must fit well. Each of the three straps adjusts: collar, girth and bellyband. Take time to get a perfect fit for each strap. Every time you use the harness, check to see if the fit of each strap is still perfect. You may decide to cut off any excess length.

COLLAR

First, adjust the collar. The fleece makes it hard to slide the webbing through the buckle, so I use a screwdriver to move the fabric through the buckle. Tuck the extra length of webbing into the sliding elastic ring to reduce the likelihood of the buckle loosening and to keep the harness looking tidy.

The collar must lie where the neck meets the body. It reaches from the junction of the neck and spine to the top of the breastbone (sternum).

To check the fit of the collar, put the harness on the dog. Put your hand through the collar with the palm up, then place your hand under the dog's chin. Hold the chin while with the other hand lift the collar over the dog's head. Settle the saddle on the dog's back. Check the fit of the collar. Touch the junction of spine and neck, does the collar sit there? Touch the top of the sternum (the end closest to the dog's throat), does the collar sit there?

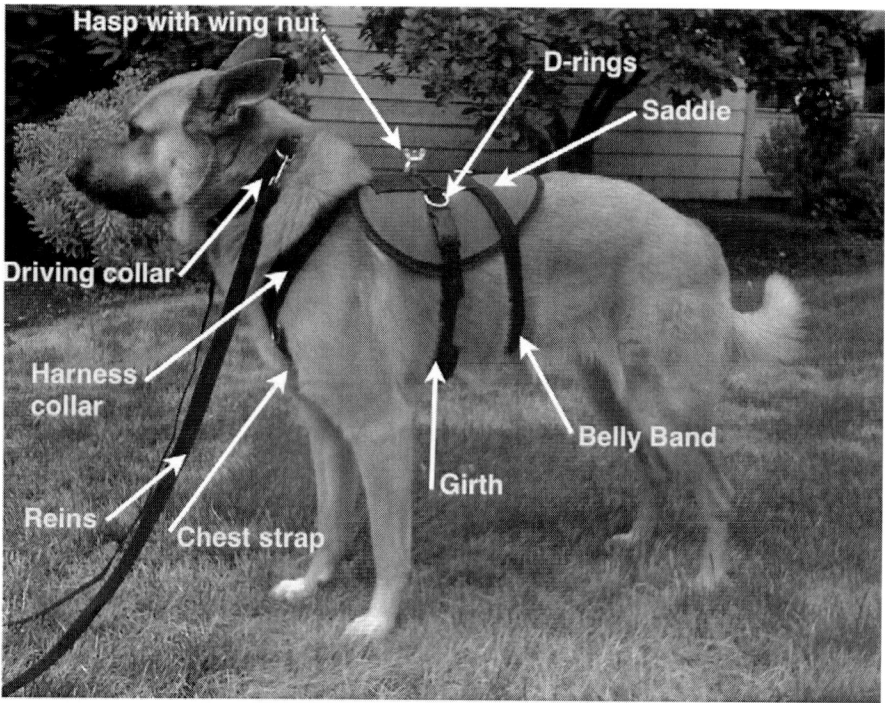

GIRTH

Once the collar fits accurately, fit the girth. Adjust it for a tight, snug fit. Think in terms of the saddle on a horse when adjusting the tightness of the girth. The girth needs to be tight to hold the collar in place so the dog does not choke when pulling. It is difficult to get the girth tight with a new harness because the saddle is stiff.

Center the chest strap on the dog's chest/sternum. Adjust the girth buckles so the two sides of the girth are the same length. I find it difficult to snap the final buckle, so I often hold the D-ring to get leverage to snap the buckle shut. As you use the harness, the saddle softens. With usage, it will be easier to snap the girth buckle shut.

Once the girth is buckled, check to be sure the chest strap is centered between the legs. It should rest squarely on the sternum.

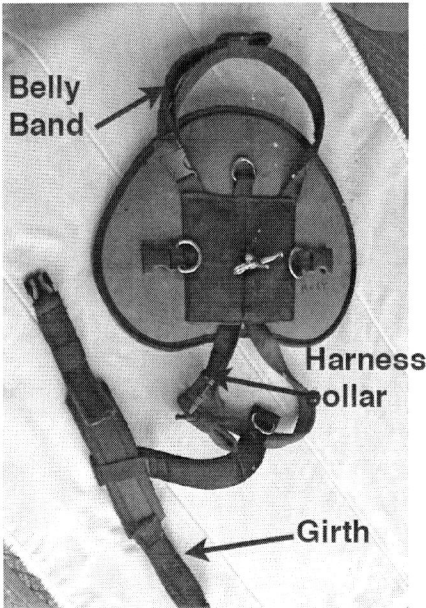

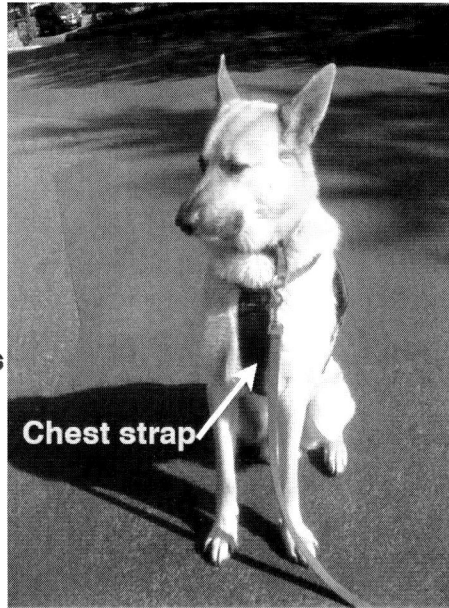

BELLYBAND

The bellyband circles the belly just behind the ribs. The bellyband does not need to be tight, so make it comfortably snug. The bellyband helps the girth to hold the saddle in place and prevents the harness from sliding over the dog's head should the sulky go faster than the dog. This happens when the dog slows down or when you drive down a slope and the sulky speeds up.

TRAINING TO PULL

Scooter dogs are often taught to pull in a casual manner. Start with hitching the dog to the scooter and have a friend stand on the scooter while you call the dog to you. The dog learns to pull the scooter while running to you. Next, ride a bike and call the dog so he chases the bike while your friend rides. This is called the rabbit method: i.e. the dog chases the rabbit. The rabbit is whatever you invent that he wants to chase. While the dog has learned that running while pulling is fun, he is far from being trained to pull on command.

The bicyclist is the rabbit that the dog is chasing.

Sulky training is more rigorous than scooter training. You may use the rabbit method at times, but mostly you need to go through rigorous ground training before riding the sulky. Since it takes a month to two months after ordering to receive a sulky, use this time to train the dog.

Dogs help two friends walk up a long hill. Leashes are snapped to the harness going uphill and to the collar going downhill.

COMMANDS/CONCEPTS

GROUND TRAINING

1. Up Front

2. Drag Training

3. Up Front and Pull

4. Line Out

5. Whoa

6. Walk, trot

7. Gee and haw

8. Reins

9. Over gee and over haw

10. On by

SULKY TRAINING

1. Introduce sulky

2. Walk with sulky

3. Dog pulls empty sulky/human walks beside him

4. Dog pulls weighted sulky/human walks beside him

5. Dog pulls weighted sulky/human walks behind sulky

6. Dog pulls sulky/human rides

7. Practice all the commands while riding the sulky

UP FRONT

"Up Front" is a useful command for more than just sulky driving. My favorite time to use "Up Front" is when hiking. I snap the leash to the harness when going uphill and tell the dog "Up Front" and then "Pull."

A dog that pulls you uphill when hiking is amazingly helpful. You go faster and easier. I don't want the dogs to pull me when I am hiking on level ground or going downhill. In those situations, I snap the leash to the collar. They are taught "Easy" when the leash is snapped to the collar. I also like

"Up Front" when I am carrying things and the sidewalk is narrow. Having them walk in front of me gets them out of my way.

"Up Front" is easier to teach with an eager young dog that hasn't learned the command "Heel" than with a dog that always walks beside you and looks to you for guidance. If you have a dog who naturally prefers to walk (or run) in front of you, couple that behavior to the "Up Front" command.

If you have a reluctant dog, a dog that stays next to you, you will have to be creative to teach him to walk in front of you on command. Perhaps at times something happens that excites your dog to walk in front of you. Perhaps the dog is excited to go to a park. When he walks in front, say, "Good dog. Good up front". Maybe a friend will walk ahead and call the dog, and the dog will move out in front of you. Your goal is for the dog to move out in front of you facing away from you when you say "Up Front."

Wait. Sit. Stay.

DRAG TRAINING

The harness is the signal to work. The dog is on duty when the leash or tug-line is snapped to the harness. When you want the dog to relax, unsnap the leash from the harness and snap it to the collar instead. Take the harness off after work is over, like when you are back in the car.

The leash is loose. The tug line is tight.

The dog needs to learn to pull <u>on command.</u> I like to use tires to teach this. The Siberian husky in the photo has been commanded to pull. His leash is loose while his tug line is tight. He likes to pull! He doesn't know "Up Front" yet.

To train the dog to pull, put on the harness. Make sure the dog accepts and is happy with the harness. The dog usually

accepts the harness right away. If the dog is unsure of the harness, check the fit. Associate the harness with fun times like going for a walk.

The next step is to teach the dog that he can go forward

even though the harness is pulling back on him. With one leash to the collar, urge the dog forward. With a second leash to the harness, pull backwards on the harness. The dog has to pull against the harness to walk forward with you.

Keep the leash to the collar loose and put backwards tension on the harness. Once the dog realizes he can move forward against pressure from the harness, have a helper walk behind and apply pressure to the

harness while you hold the leash to the collar. Tell the dog "Pull" and trot along beside the dog. If he lunges ahead, tell him good dog and drop behind him so he learns to pull out in front of you like the Doberman in the photo above.

These small poodles understand how to pull. Their owner practices pulling on command while walking behind. These poodles are warming up to compete in weight pull.

Up FRONT AND PULL

Next, combine "Up Front" with "Pull." Having the dogs pull

tires is a practical way to teach pulling. I like bicycle tires because I can add more tires as the dogs get stronger. I have a flexi-lead attached to a neckline that connects them. I enjoy tire-pulling because I get exercise along with the dogs. Many people tire pull at the beginning of training only, but I use it as a fun way to take a walk. Hard-pulling dogs pull the tire and not my arm. A tire walk fatigues the dogs more than a walk without a tire. After a while, it is second nature to a dog to face forward, stay out in front of you and pull with his harness.

Tire-pulling allows you to train commands, and because you are on foot, you are able to show the dog what you want and you can enforce the command. When you have a problem when driving your sulky, go back to tire training. Hitch the dogs to the tires and go for a pull. You can more easily correct the dogs when you are on foot than when you are riding in the sulky.

Tire-pulling builds stamina and strength. I like to cut my bike tires (not shown in photos) so if they catch on a root or rock, they slide along without jerking the dog abruptly.

My dogs and I vary the kinds of pulling we do. Sometimes we pull tires on a long walk, and sometimes we dash around on scooters. Other times we drive sulkies. We also pull the wagon full of clothes to the Laundromat and the groceries home with the TrailDog.

LINE OUT

Dogs must not turn and face you when hitched to the sulky. After you hitch them, they must remain facing away from the sulky while you walk back to the sulky to sit on it. To stand still and face away becomes a work habit.

In this photo, dogs are learning "Line Out." They are attached to a fence by their tug line. They learn to walk away from the fence until the line is tight and then to stand still holding the line out tight. Even though the sulky has an aluminum shaft instead of a line, the dog needs a command that means "Face forward away from the sulky and stay there."

Some people teach this command with the leash, and some people use treats. Most use a combination.

I enjoy watching my dogs line out. On Sundays we scooter through a hunting and fishing park. I place the scooter and call the dogs out of the car one at a time. Then I snap the tug line to their harnesses. They stand watching while I shut the car doors and lock them. I hold the handlebars and say "Line out." The dogs face away from me and hold the line tight. Then I say "Pull." It is really cool!

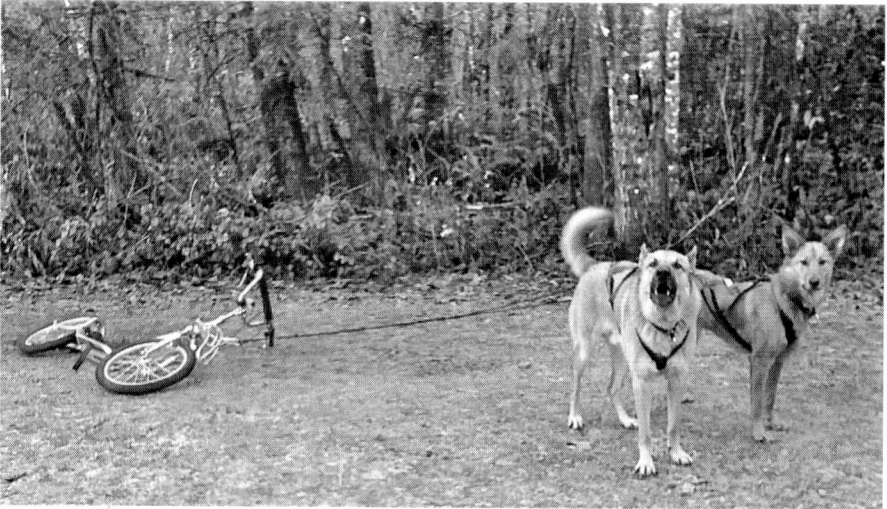

Even dogs so excited to go for a run that they bark can line out.

WHOA

The dog must stop when you command "Whoa" (or "Wait"). Dragging tires and having the flexi-lead attached to the collar makes it easy to teach and enforce "Whoa." When I tire train, my dogs wear prong collars. Prong collars are more effective than buckle collars and do not damage the dog's throat when pulled on for corrections. Dogs respond quickly to prong collars. My trainer years ago called them "power steering."

The Simple Sulky has no brakes. If you are driving on level ground, you can tell the dog "Whoa," and he will be able to stop the sulky himself. When I wish to stop, I first tell my trotting dogs to slow down to a walk. Then a little later, I tell them to "Wait." It is easier for them to stop a slow sulky than a fast one, and they are less likely to tear their pads. I find that the dog does the braking even with the chalo sulky with brakes—especially since I often ride with a video camera in the hand that controls the brake lever.

A well-trained sulky dog plus your foot dragging on the ground stops the sulky well enough. I brace one foot on the footrest and place the sole of my shoe on the ground to stop my sulky.

When going downhill, I dismount the sulky and walk beside the dog to keep the sulky from pushing into him and scaring him. It depends of course on the steepness and length of the hill, whether it is dirt or pavement and the size and the ability of the dog.

WALK AND TROT

One of the thrills of driving a dog sulky is the teamwork—it is like having a dance partner! You need to be able to tell your dog to move at a walk or trot depending on circumstances. You can teach the commands while walking on leash. Once the dog seems to know to change pace on command, try it while he is pulling tires. You are successful when he will walk or trot on command while you walk or trot behind the tires he is pulling.

You may want to teach him to go fast on command. A dog loping is faster than I can run. If you are slow like me, you will need to teach "go fast" while driving the sulky. Figure out when the dog is likely to pick up speed and attach a word to that. We used to see rabbits along one of our trails, and dogs speed up when they see rabbits. My word for "run fast" is "RABBITS!" said of course with enthusiasm. I now have several speed up words such as "YES, YES, YES!", "RABBITS!", "SQUIRRELS!" and "HIKE!"

GEE AND HAW (RIGHT AND LEFT)

Some people teach Gee and Haw on the couch inside their house. They hold the dog between their knees facing away from the couch. They hold a treat out to the right and say "Gee!" Dog turns his head toward the treat and gets it. And this goes on until the dog turns his head to the right whenever you say "Gee." Continue training by increasing the distance the dog has to move when you say "Gee."

Whenever you take a walk with the dog, say "Gee" just before you turn right. Say "Haw" just before you turn left.

Once the dog understands the words, hitch him to the tires. Practice the Gee/Haw commands along with the other commands.

REINS

Reins allow you to steer the dog precisely. A trained sulky dog responds to very slight pressure from the reins.

I started in the sport of dog pulling by scootering with my Rottweiler, Rubromarginata. When pulling a scooter, he was perfect at turning on command. Because of his perfect gee/haw commands with a scooter, I thought that I didn't need reins when driving a sulky. I hit a curb on the very first Gee without reins.

With a scooter, you steer independently of the dog. Tell the dog "Gee," and he gees around the tree. You gee around the tree a bit later than the dog does. With a sulky, you tell the dog Gee and the sulky follows right behind him. He is the car. The sulky is its trailer.

To train the reins, snap the driving collar to the dog and attach the reins. Walk behind the dog and perhaps behind the sulky. Practice commands such as gee and haw, stop and start and gee over and haw over. The dog knows these commands verbally, and soon he will know them from the reins.

OVER GEE AND OVER HAW

Sulkies usually drive on multi-use trails. They need to drive on the right-hand side of the trail to go with the traffic. "Over Gee" means move over to the right side of the trail. "Over haw" means move over to the left side of the trail. Use "Over Haw" when you need to pull to the left to pass a pedestrian. If the trail is narrow and other users come along, be polite. Pull over to the side and give them room to walk past. Many people are afraid of dogs. Never give other trail users an excuse to get dog drivers removed from the list of acceptable users.

To train "Over Haw," take your dog for a walk, preferably while pulling a tire so he knows he is working. Walk along on the right-hand side of the trail for a while and then say, "Over Haw." Walk in a long diagonal to the far left of the trail. Continue there for a while, then say "Over Gee" and walk in a long diagonal to the right-hand edge of the trail and so forth.

ON BY

"On By" is short for "Go on by the distraction." In a pinch, you can belt out "Leave it!" or "No," but "On By" is better because it tells the dog what to do. "Leave it" and "No" tell the dog what *not* to do. The dog must go on by distractions like bushes to pee on, trails that look fun and especially loose dogs. Many people out walking their dogs are accustomed to telling people that their dog is friendly and would like to say hi. Tell these people that your dog is working, and he is not allowed to say hi when working.

When they are trotting along pulling the sulky, my dogs go "On By" dogs on the leash and dogs off the leash.

Sulky Training

1. Introduce Sulky

2. Walk with Sulky

3. Dog pulls empty sulky—human walks beside him

4. Dog pulls weighted sulky—human walks beside him

5. Dog pulls weighted sulky—human walks behind sulky

6. Dog pulls sulky—human rides

7. Practice all the commands while riding the sulky

1. INTRODUCE SULKY

It is difficult to change a dog's mind once they develop fear of wheeled vehicles. Train slowly, anticipate a fearful situation and avoid it, or introduce the situation carefully. My Rosy was hit by a car, and now she is frightened of things behind her. She is frightened of noises like brakes squeaking or shoes dragging on gravel. Before the accident, she was a fine scooter and bike dog. She enjoyed pulling and she ran hard. Since the accident, she will go along just fine for a while, and then suddenly will pull backwards against the other dog. She looks fearfully at me. It is far easier to train slowly and carefully than it is to correct mistakes later.

Introduce the sulky to the dog; show him the wheels, the shaft, the seat, everything. Invite him to sniff the sulky. Hide treats in it. Bang it a bit and shake it. Some people store it in the living room so the dog can get used to it. Some people even feed their dogs next to the sulky. Some people get excited, "Look, dog, look at the sulky! Oh boy, this is a sulky," and they tap the sulky and treats fall from it. Have fun...

2.   WALK WITH SULKY

Once the dog is fine with the stationary sulky, go for a walk. Put the dog on the leash and walk while you pull the sulky. Walk on various surfaces. Walk on pavement, grass, gravel, cobbles, and leaves. Go over bumps so the sulky will make different sounds. You want the dog to decide that the sulky is not going to hurt him no matter what sounds it makes. When he and the sulky are together, it is fun. He gets to move on down the trail and go someplace.

You have to decide how many times you need to take a walk while you pull the sulky. Some really confident dogs pay little attention to the sulky, and you can move to the next stage right away. Other dogs, like my Rosy, need several walks to overcome their fear.

3.   DOG PULLS EMPTY SULKY/HUMAN WALKS BESIDE HIM

Hitch the dog to the sulky and go for a walk. Hang a weight from the cargo bar so the shaft lifts up slightly. If you don't hang a weight, the shaft tip may cause the harness to slip to one side. It depends on the shape of the dog, the slipperiness of his hair, and how tight you can make the girth. If the harness doesn't slip to one side, you don't need to weight the cargo bar.

On this initial walk, the dog needs to learn that it is OK that something is following him. The pull on the harness is a bit different from the pull of the training tires. Walk in level easy areas until the dog walks with no concern for the sulky traveling behind him. Many trainers feel that short fun walks are best. In other words, it may be well worth your while to continue these short fun walks with nothing scary for several days. You can add command training as the walks continue. Practice "Whoa," turns and changes of pace.

A Rottweiler is ground training with the spyder sulky.

Once the dog is completely easy with pulling the empty sulky on level smooth ground, lengthen the walks and travel on gravel, grass and bumpy trails.

A target is a place that the dog wants to go to. A lake for swimming and chasing sticks would be a fine target. A place where the dog can run off leash is also a fine target. Perhaps you will play fetch the stick there. If free play is not possible, you can unhitch the dog and let him sniff and walk around while you hold one end of the reins. The reins are much longer than a leash. After you re-hitch him to the sulky, give him treats. I like to save the best treats for this training—the high-value treats.

My car is a target. When they get to the car, they get chicken jerky. They sit at the van cargo door facing me. I break the jerky into small pieces and give it to them multiple times. "Good Rosy," "Good Brett," over and over. I want the word "good" to be a strong reinforcement.

We go to our TARGET, the park, where I throw the fetch toys in my bag. The dogs happily pull their tires.

Be careful at all times not to scare the dog. For example, don't let the wheels catch on curbs or bollards and jerk him in the harness. One trainer I know will walk her dog along and will artificially jerk the dog. In other words, she pulls back on the sulky in a jerky way and thereby gets the dog accustomed to it. With her kind of acclimation, when the dog is jerked in real life, it is no big deal.

I had a dog that was afraid of the sulky. I took her on long training drive over hill and dale. I figured with this much exposure, she would get over her fear. She was afraid of driving between the bollards. I slowed way down to drive safely between the bollards, but at the end of the run, I caught a wheel on one of the many sets of bollards we drove through. This frightened her all over again. My carelessness at the end of the run negated the training run.

4. DOG PULLS WEIGHTED SULKY/HUMAN WALKS BESIDE HIM

Now it is time to build the dog's strength and confidence. You can gradually add weight to the seat of the sulky and have the dog practice starting and stopping. He will learn to lean into the harness to start the sulky. Try walking some hills. You will probably need to hold the sulky back on the downhills with your hand on the shaft.

The final weight on the seat will be equal to your weight. That way when you get on the sulky, he will already know how to pull that much weight.

With each additional weight, adjust the seat so that the shaft lifts on the dog's harness by 10 or 15 pounds.

Once the dog is pulling the weighted sulky with confidence, you can begin training him to the reins. Practice turns and stops with the reins as communication.

5. DOG PULLS SULKY/HUMAN WALKS BEHIND SULKY

Harness the dog. Fasten the weights in the seat. Attach the reins. Drive him while you walk behind the sulky.

Do this until you and he are both confident and working well together. A week of ground driving should be enough time and training. Practice all the commands including Trot and Walk. Once you tell him Trot, he should continue trotting until you say "Easy" or "Walk." The same holds true with Whoa or Wait. When you tell the dog "Whoa," he should slow down, stop and face forward until you tell him to do something else.

Warning — When you get to a destination such as a coffee shop or grocery store, unhitch the dog. Do not leave him hitched to the sulky. Something could happen that causes him to run and flip the sulky, scaring himself. You will have lost your fine confident dog in a one-minute mistake. Also, be aware that people, especially children, climb into empty sulkies. The sulky then tips over and the person is hurt. Find a solution to this hazard. It could be a sign "Do not sit in sulky," turning the sulky upside down or tying the shaft tip to a bike rack.

The husband rides his bike. The wife trains her service dog. The teamwork is great.

6.   DOG PULLS SULKY/HUMAN RIDES

You have done all this preparation. The dog is ready. At last it is time for your first ride. Choose a safe, easy and familiar route. First rides are usually short. Sometimes people combine the first ride with spells of walking beside the sulky. Sometimes people enlist the support of spouses or friends. In the photograph, a husband rides his bicycle cheering the dog on while his wife drives her service dog.

7.   PRACTICE ALL THE COMMANDS WHILE RIDING THE SULKY

Training continues once you start driving. In fact, it may increase as you switch from walking to driving. You will be traveling farther and faster than you could when walking. On every drive, something happens that tells you what further training is needed. Be prepared to jump out of the sulky and firmly correct your dog.

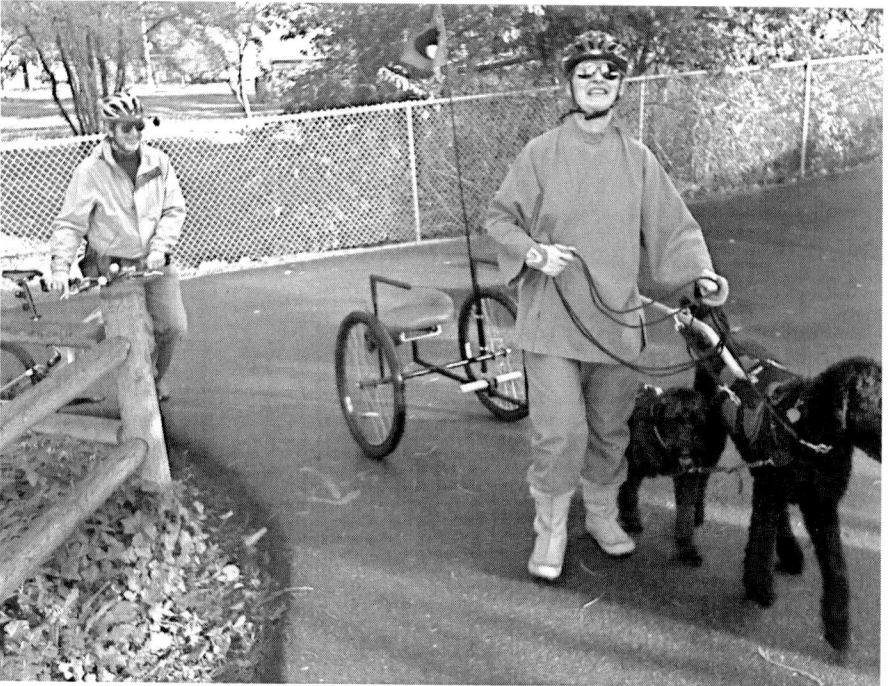

That first successful drive is a thrill! Look at the smiles.

Dogs are capable of amazing athleticism. At first, driving a few blocks or a mile will be a big accomplishment. For most dogs as they become fit, 10 miles on a drive is reasonable. I know of a Great Dane that pulls his scooter 10 to 20 miles on his outings.

Check your dog's feet after a drive. If you see a pink color showing through the pads, the grey protective coating has worn down. Rest the feet for a few days for the grey to grow back, and consider having your dog wear booties. If you can find trails that are not paved, that is better for the dog's feet and joints according to mushers.

Sulky Adjustment

UNDERSTAND BALANCE

The dorsal hitch sulky is designed to lift upwards on the dog's harness. The upward lift should slightly raise the harness off the dog's back. This lift occurs when you sit in the seat. Think of a lever or think of a seesaw. When you aren't seated, the shaft tip rests on the harness. On some dogs, this causes the harness to slip to one side as in the photo below.

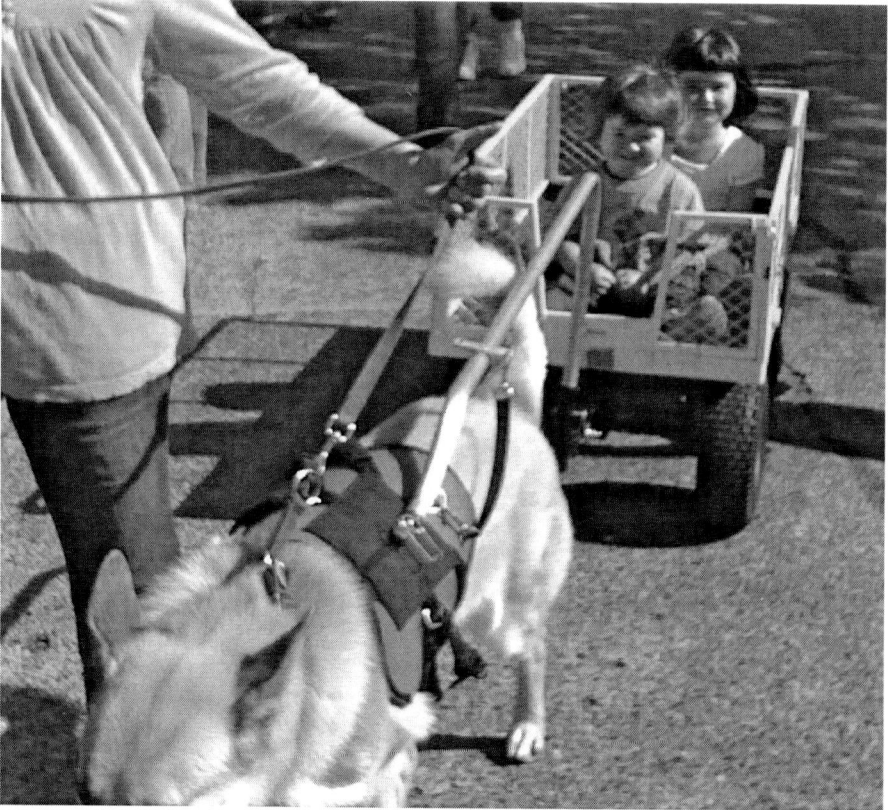

Remember to check tire pressure at least once a week. Keep the tires at 50 pounds to make it easy for your dog to pull.

ADJUST THE SULKY FOR PROPER LIFT TO THE SHAFT TIP

Once you get your harness fitted to your dog, fit the sulky to you and the dog. You need a helper to hold the shaft tip while you adjust various parts of the sulky.

HEIGHT OF FORWARD SHAFT

The forward shaft (the aluminum one) slides up and down in the rear shaft. Determine the best hole into which to insert the wire pin. Choose the hole that allows the rear shaft to be horizontal when the shaft tip is attached to the harnessed dog.

POSITION OF FOOT REST

Sit in the seat with your helper holding the shaft tip. Determine the most comfortable location for the footrest given the length of your legs. Slide the footrest to that position and secure it. The footrest can locate above or below the rear shaft.

POSITION OF SEAT

Now adjust the seat. Again, have your helper hold the shaft tip while you sit in the seat. There should be an upward lift of 10 to 15 pounds on his/her hand. Use the Garelick seat slider to adjust the seat back and forth until you have a good upward lift—not too much and not too little. You may need to adjust the footrest again.

Happy and safe driving to you!

Feel free to call if you have questions.

Daphne Lewis

206-304-7390

daphne@chalosulky.com

www.chalosulky.com